The Lonely Only

The Triumphs and Tragedy of Raising Bi-Racial Children in Texas

By Sonya Washington

III Coaching, Austin, Texas

The Lonely Only
The Triumphs and Tragedy of Raising Bi-Racial Children in Texas

Copyright © 2022 by Sonya Washington

ISBN: 9798818876207

Cover Design by Shamim Rashid
Edited by Lauren Sophie

Published by III Coaching
https://www.coreytabor.com/iiicoaching

Dedication

I dedicate this book to the lights of my life, my sons.

You have brought unbelievable joy to my heart and soul.

Run through every obstacle and let nothing stop you from achieving your goals.

Sonya W. (AKA, your mom)

Table of Contents

Introduction

When I first sat down to write this book, I never imagined I would actually ever finish it. Before I really had any sort of direction, I decided to share my whole self with my word processor, unloading story after story into a blank document, not knowing how all the pieces would eventually fall together.

But you know what? Those first few months watching the document grow larger and larger became one of the most gratifying periods of my life. I felt like I was lifting my memories and carefully slotting them into these very pages. When I would step back and look over my work, I realized these stories were about so much more than tales immortalizing the young men I raised and their path to maturity; this is a chronicling of my path to maturity as well.

But as large projects often do, this one also reached its inevitable conclusion, and as I neared that day, the need for this book became even greater. The George Floyd incident of 2020 reawakened something in me I thought I wouldn't feel again now that my boys are men. The incident made me feel a kind of vulnerability, a kind of helplessness not set on me by anyone but by an entire society. And so, I wrote. I wrote, and I wrote, and

I wrote, hoping that finding the words to say would distract me from all of the anguish and hurt in my world.

The world has a way of reminding us of how alone we are, often when we least want to hear it. When I see people who look like me and my boys ostracized by civilians or targeted by police, that helplessness is magnified. When I look to the news and see other families suffering, scared, or displaced by a sometimes-uncaring population, I yearn for a way to reach out to them.

So, as I captured my family's story in this book, I wanted "The Lonely Only" to serve not so much as a guide but as a loose set of testimonies to the triumph and tragedy of raising bi-racial children in the heart of Texas. I want you to feel my outrage, determination, heartbreak, and everything, and I want you to know that you are not alone in your personal journey. Even more than that, I hope you are able to dip your cup and drink from the fountain of my experience. And if there is only one lesson you glean from the pages of this book, it would be that no matter what this world throws at us, says to us, or does to us, our greatest strength comes from our ability to be alone together.

Chapter 1
The Beginning
A Family Grows Larger

"When a child is born the mother also is born again."
--Gilbert Parker (1913). "The lane that had no turning and other
associated tales concerning the people of Pontiac. Parables of a
province"

It's Halloween dress up day at the office. A freshly hired training teacher, I am determined to dress up with my class and enjoy the day's festivities at the office, no matter what.

My costume is a McDonald's Big Mac -- the perfect costume for me and my 7.5-month-pregnant belly. Pulling into the office, I notice an urge to go to the restroom, but with class starting in just a few minutes, there's no way I'll make it with time to spare.

"You need to get the projector set up," I think to myself as I do a part jog, part waddle through the hallways. "What's the computer password again?"

But when nature calls, it stays calling. Deciding I would simply apologize profusely to the students for the late start, I give in and make a b-line for the restroom.

After bolting to the restroom, I'm surprised to find slight dampness in my pants. Bewildered, I return to my car to gather my thoughts and see what I could do. There's no chance of me showing up to class on time now. Stepping out into the parking lot, I catch sight of Rhonda, a mother of five and a friend to me in my short time working here. I'm not exactly sure how we met, but believe me, I'll never forget this conversation.

"Is this normal?" I ask after frantically explaining what I'm going through. "Do you maybe have a panty liner I can borrow?" I'm beyond determined to get through the work day.

"Nooo, sweetie, that's your water," she replies.

"Whatttt?" I cry out uncomprehending, especially since I didn't feel anything amounting to a labor contraction. "No, no, no, no. He's not due till December 5th! What are you talking about? I'm having a snowflake, not a pumpkin."

"I need to get you to a doctor," Rhonda says before placing a call to my husband and whisking me away to the hospital, her car going as fast as it could go.

My husband meets me at the hospital. After what feels like hours but, in reality, is just minutes, I sit on the examining table, and the nursing staff confirms that, yes, my water has broken and I need to be admitted to the hospital.

I make the momma phone call, and she's in disbelief. We're a month and a half early, but she needs to get on the road. Ohhh, how exciting! My first baby!!

The next eight hours are a blur of screaming, pushing, nurses screaming at me to push, and a smattering of more delivery room chaos. The next thing I remember with clarity was two simple words: He's here.

I'm tired but elated with my husband. I remember thinking, "let me see! My God, let me see. I want to hold him, my baby, whom I've been on this eight-month journey with."

I hear excited chatter and see smiles. Something about his hair and eyes. As my husband cuts the cord, he looks up at me excitedly. "He has golden blonde hair and blue eyes," he says.

To his surprise, and a bit to mine also, my face did not register the same excitement. The nurses immediately take my new baby boy to the scale and wrap him tightly in a blanket. "5 pounds, 16 ounces, slightly under six pounds!" A nurse calls out.

At long last, the nurse is coming towards me with my baby, every step seemingly taken in slow motion. There, amidst all the delivery room chaos, I catch the first glimpse of my first boy. He has all the characteristics of a Caucasian baby, solid yellow gold straight hair, aqua blue eyes, and pinkish flushed skin.

I suppose the nurse took notice that I didn't reach for him right away. "Do you want to hold him?" She asks, but I can only shake my head "no." With everything happening so quickly, my mind is a whir of leftover sedatives, delivery room noise, and more questions than I can handle right now. Where's my momma? What just happened? Why doesn't my baby look anything like me? Did I fail to keep my bun in the oven long enough? How?

I was in such disbelief that literally if I wasn't in a hospital with my family by my side, no one could have convinced me that was my baby. You see, growing up in my neighborhood, I had only met one or two bi-racial kids, and on TV, I had only seen one or two bi-racial celebrities, and they were Halle Berry and Derek Jeter. I had assumed that, of course, my child would be no different.

About this time, my cousin, Shawna, comes over to the side of the bed to check on me. "Cousin, you okay?" She asks, rubbing my hair softly.

"He looks just like Eric," I say with a confused look on my face. Shawna chuckles softly and continues stroking my hair. "Cousin, your doctor didn't tell you your baby could be white or black?"

"Huh? Uh, no," I say. "I thought black genes always dominated and that he would have dark hair, eyes, and some of my skin tone…"

"Oh, sometimes. But Eric's genes must have been more dominant," Shawna says.

I look over at the incubator with curiosity, and Shawna asks if I want to hold him again. I say yes, and the nurse overhears and brings him over.

This time it's different. We have our moment. I look in his eyes, feel his warmth, love transfers between us, and know this is my angel, and I will protect him for all the days of my life. And from that moment on, I did not want my baby boy out of my sight.

A couple of hours later, Mom and dad made it, which completed the day. Lots of visitors, family and loved ones stop by the room to see the new edition. I'm in love more and more each day. I'm so exhausted I agree to him sleeping in the nursery the first night. The next morning, I awake in disbelief that I had done it…I'm a mom; my baby boy is down the hall.

Suddenly, I hear a knock at the door. "Come in," I call, and the door opens to reveal the nurse toting the baby carrier. I start to beam with joy and happiness. But as the nurse enters, she makes eye contact with me and begins to back out of the room.

"Oh, I'm sorry," she says quickly, leaving me completely confused as to what's going on. Then it hits me. Without checking first, this nurse made an assumption based on the color of my and my baby's skin and decided I wasn't his mommy. I saw his face and knew that was my baby…. "Wait," I cry out, trying to raise myself in my bed. "Excuse me. Is that Eric Christian Worden, blonde hair, blue eyes, with a tiny scratch on the cheek? That's my baby!"

The nurse slowly re-enters the room and pauses at the foot of my bed. "Oh, I'm so sorry," she says, checking my hospital bracelet before handing baby Eric to me and leaving the room.

Up until that point in my life, I had never been more horrified. She had seen me, Eric's mother, and she was walking away with my baby. My baby.

I knew from that moment on there would be no more trips to the nursery, and daddy must accompany him on all necessary visits. It began to occur to me that this was our new normal, of not being like everyone else -- me, an African-American woman, and my darling blond-haired, blue-eyed bi-racial baby Eric. No, I had never experienced this cocktail of emotions before, but Eric was mine. That was a certainty. Even then, lying there cradling him close, I couldn't even begin to imagine the experiences that would come to shape his young life, completely transforming us both in the process.

Chapter 2
Getting Hurt
Strangers Can Be Hurtful, but It's Family That Cuts the Deepest

"I believe that one can never leave home. I believe that one carries the shadows, the dreams, the fears and the dragons of home under one's skin, at the extreme corners of one's eyes and possibly in the gristle of the earlobe."
Maya Angelou (2008). "Letter to My Daughter", p.7, Random House

I excitedly dote over baby Eric, carefully bundling him up for a trip to the grocery store where I'll start preparations for Eric's first Thanksgiving.

"Your first Thanksgiving, baby Eric," I think to myself, tossing another couple of blankets in the baby carrier, so he doesn't catch a draft. I'm in that proud new mommy mode, eager to give thanks for my recent bundle of joy with his aunt, uncle, grandparents, and cousins all together.

I only need a few things to complete our Thanksgiving dinner menu, so I don't expect to be in the store for long. "All set, new mommy in motion," I say to myself as we make our way inside, Eric safe and snug in his carrier.

I get a few smiles from a few shoppers who notice my bundle onboard. We begin to head through the bakery when an elderly African American gentleman approaches.

"Hey, what do you got there?" He asks. "My newborn baby boy," I reply, trying to move us along.

"Congratulations," he says, and I think briefly that's the end of it. "Can I take a peek?" He asks.

I hesitate but decide a quick glance won't hurt. I don't want to be rude. So, I slightly pull the blanket back to reveal baby Eric, wide awake.

The man chuckles. "Gurllll, stop it, you know that ain't your baby," he says. "Who are you babysitting?"

"Yes, this is my baby boy," I say, confused while the man just continues laughing and waving his arms.

"Who are you?" He continues to interrogate. "The nanny? The babysitter?"

I stop trying to explain as my eyes begin to well, my throat tightening and my heart aching from pure hurt. I cover my baby up again, utterly devastated and in genuine shock. I walk away from the man and finish my shopping, but I can't stop the tears from cascading down my face.

I'm still fighting to keep my composure as I load baby Eric back into the car, the trip's experience already embedding itself in my memory. "I am your mommy," I say over and over. "I am your mommy, and I love you so much."

My goal from the beginning has been to surround my sons with the love of family, just as I was raised. It was important that they always had a sense of belonging no matter what the world dealt them. I wanted to make sure they learned about and equally understood their black and white heritage.

Most of all, I didn't want them growing up feeling like they had to choose.

While I have countless cousins, aunts, and uncles, it wasn't quite the same on their father's side of the family. Their paternal grandfather decided to disown his family, never to associate with them again. Meanwhile, their paternal grandmother was adopted and didn't have a relationship with her adoptive family beyond her childhood. I wanted to make sure family was foremost in my children's lives.

Over 70 years ago, on Clifford Avenue, two brothers decided to buy homes next door to each other. One of the brothers was my grandfather, who I would come to call Papa. Both homes remain in the family to this day and are occupied by the children of my grandfather and his brother's children. My family's traditions run deep, and they've done so for over 70 years. Clifford, you see, is a place where the doors are never locked, there's always plenty of food, and there are no fences, leaving the kids free to run back and forth between the two houses. For 70 years, here is where my family learned to eat together, play together, cook together, work together, love each other, and support each other.

Everyone goes to church on Sunday mornings. It doesn't matter if you live there or are just visiting one of the Clifford houses. And afterward, my uncles will always have Sunday dinner ready with enough food to feed fifteen or twenty people. The menu will usually consist of three meats, four vegetables, and without fail, my uncle's 7-Up cake. I grew up here, visiting every summer, attending family reunions, and going to the Baptist Association with my Papa, who was famously known for his BBQ and red water. So, Sundays on Clifford was a way I could share that piece of my past with my children.

The house is always open with only the glass screen door closed. You can usually find one or two cousins or uncles sitting on the porch or in the field behind the house. My uncles would never ask anyone to bring anything. They would always find a way. Some days, it would be eight, some days, it would be twenty, but my aunts and uncles would make sure there was always enough food for everyone to be full.

Here is where my kids bonded with all their cousins, from walking to the corner store, running to the ice cream truck, shooting basketball at the hoop in the backyard, to just playing chase around the yard. Once a year, on the first weekend of August, the entire family would come together for a family reunion. Despite our busy baseball schedule, we would always make time. The field that stretched across the back of both homes on Clifford served as our multi-purpose gathering spot. Besides our family reunion gathering spot, this was also our venue for birthdays, holiday cookouts, and shade tree bonding. Starting Friday evening and not letting up through Sunday evening, there would be continuous music, moonwalks, volleyball, basketball, dancing, dominoes, cards, and hundreds of family members just letting loose. Being with family was always so fulfilling for me, and I could only hope my sons were absorbing a small portion of it.

But even here, amongst family, we can't fully escape the 'lonely only' comments. There will always be some small comment or incident that serves to remind me that my kids are of two cultures.

By this time, my second son had come along, and I remember the kids being about 2 and 4 as we walked up to the field to join the family behind my grandma's house. I can hear my cousin loudly say, 'oh, here come my white cousins.' Another relative says, 'oh, there go, Buffy and Jody, my nephews.' Another family member would greet them by saying, 'what's up my n-word…'

While it was a joke to them, it was exhausting and ridiculous to me. How often did I say my kids are bi-racial repeatedly and don't call them that? Over time, those jokes became hurtful to my boys and led to some internal confusion for them. When they were still small, I sensed a hesitance from them when it came to those family visits. I knew it would be easy to just avoid those family members and any functions where they would be present, but I knew that was not the right choice for my boys and their future.

Instead, I began having important conversations with them both at an early age, preparing them for a world that might not always have something nice to say.

Luckily, through the years and many conversations, both Eric and Alec have developed amazing patience, coming to understand appropriate things to say to bi-racial children, along with an understanding that not everyone will say appropriate things. They've come to understand that despite that, we still love our family members no matter what.

I always made it a point to redirect and correct my sons' behavior if I saw it out of control. Many might say I was a hovering mom or a 'helicopter mom,' but I don't care. The men I see today make all of that worth it. These are men who are driven, caring, respectful of all, empathetic, and armed with the knowledge that no one is the lesser man; we are all God's children. But it took a number of important lessons and setbacks to develop such an informed understanding for all of us -- some big, some small.

May your family always remain whole. May you all remember that loss and disagreements are but temporary things. A family, at its core, is a tapestry of connected spirits. May your tapestry stay beautiful forever.

--Sonya' W

Chapter 3
Picture Day
We are a family and don't you forget

"Perhaps it is impossible for a person who does no good to do no harm."

--Harriet Beecher Stowe

We're up early on a Saturday for what will be my weekend life for the next eight years. The younger boys (six and nine) both have little league practice this morning, and its picture day.

"You can't miss picture day," I coo excitedly as I bounce from room to room, ensuring teeth are brushed, socks are matching, and bellies are full. "I can't wait to show your grandparents."

Everybody is running through the house trying to make it to the field with an hour to spare before game time per the coach's instructions.

"Go ahead and just get them there on time, and I'll head over shortly," I tell their dad. With the boys on their way, I run upstairs and find my baseball mom shaker and team hat. Nothing like supporting my boys in style.

Before I can get out of the house, the phone rings. It's their dad wondering where I am. "Hurry, we're going to take team pictures now," he says urgently. Panicking slightly, I hop in the car and race to the field, making the usual five-minute journey feel like less than two.

I hop off the car, running through the field, scanning for a mass gathering of spiffily-dressed baseball players. As I find my boys, it dons on me that I've missed the team and individual picture sessions. I feel my heart sink in disappointment.

Then, I catch sight of the boys' dad through the crowd and early morning fog, order form in hand. Great, I think to myself, at least I made it in time for us to choose our photos together. I'm sure he isn't excited because I always want to order everything.

"Hey, babe, what have you got so far?" I ask, sidling up beside him. He explained that he spoke with the photographer and asked if we could order pictures for both boys on the same form, which is always great and less of a headache for us. Thankfully, the photographer agreed.

So here we are, standing side by side, looking at the picture order form. I'm excitedly pointing out things, naturally.

"Baby, you need some lotion," my husband suddenly says, which I'll admit threw me off my game for a second. After all, here I was racing like a chicken with its head cut off trying to get these kids out of the house in presentable outfits, and all this man could talk about is that I need lotion?

"Oh, leave me alone," I say dismissively, taking my eyes away from him and back to the photo order form.

I hear a voice call out suddenly. "Good morning." I glance up briefly and give the approaching photographer a cheery smile before returning my attention to the order form.

"Will you be ordering pictures today?" The photographer asks, getting closer to us, my husband never taking his eyes off the form either.

"Oh, yes," I respond, pointing to the form. "We'll just order here for both of the boys."

There's a pause as the photographer seems to be processing what I just said, as if it were some kind of complicated calculus problem I had just thrown at him. "No," he finally says. "It's one order per form. You'll need your own form."

"I thought we could order for both boys on the same form?" I ask, a little heat rushing to my cheeks. It had been a long morning already, and I wasn't ready for a photographer to test me so.

"No, only one order per form," he says again, and it's about this time I realize this photographer thinks my white husband and I are here for two different sets of kids. The little heat in my cheeks suddenly feels like a fully cranked furnace.

"This is my husband," I say deliberately and slowly. "We have two sons who play on this team. Now, do we need a separate form?"

Without so much as an apology, the photographer mutters that we're fine and shuffles away, leaving me hurt and dumbfounded.

I'm sure that photographer had scanned over the team and, not seeing anyone who looked like me, decided I was trying to pull one over on his fancy photo operation. I couldn't believe it. Suddenly, all the wind had been taken out of my sails. "Just order what you want. I'm going to the car," I tell my husband before turning on my heel.

Let your love for your family and those around you shield you when strangers freely cast the arrows of judgment. For those arrows that penetrate your armor, choose the healing of family over the satisfaction of revenge.

--Sonya' W.

Chapter 4
When in Brenham
When the World is Unkind, Take a Stand

It's another Saturday at the ballpark as part of a tournament weekend in Brenham, Texas. The car is loaded with everything the family could possibly need for a day full of baseball -- gear and drinks for the boys and chairs for me and my husband. For the past ten years, this has been our normal, every Saturday and Sunday.

We sit in the parking lot waiting to brave Texas' signature humid summer temperatures and for the game to kick off. By now, both of our boys are old enough to drive, but supporting them and their game is just what we do. So we are a bit of a rarity as we finally make our way to the field. As game time approaches, I grab my chair and mini cooler, walk to the stadium bleachers and find myself a nice shady spot away from other parents.

The game gets off to a nice start. We knock in a few hits and runs to cushion a nice lead. Eric is on third, and Alec is on second; yes, they are both on the same team, a baseball mom's dream. A couple of innings go by, and the opposing team has put a little hitting streak together and starts to close the lead. Our pitcher is struggling to close out the game.

Coach has seen enough and heads to the mound. He nods for Eric to come to the mound and close the game. We applaud the leaving pitcher and wait with anticipation as Eric approaches and begins to warm up.

Faintly, out of the jitters and cheers of the crowd, I can faintly make out another noise, a noise that I definitely should not be hearing.

"Do you hear that?" I ask my husband, nudging him.

"Hear what?" He asks quizzically.

Then, the noises get louder. As Eric proceeds to wind up and send a pitch, the opposing stands erupt in a cacophony of monkey sounds.

"OOooh-eee, ah-ah," some of the spectators chanted, and the noise was getting louder with every passing pitch.

Incensed, I jumped to my feet, a hot burning in my cheeks as I took up a position behind the opposing team's dugout. I could feel the spectators' eyes on me as they wondered what this angry-looking woman was doing behind the dugout. But I was done explaining myself to anyone.

I waited behind that dugout for the rest of the game, ready to confront the coach as soon as the game had concluded. By this time, my husband had joined me as well.

"Hi there, can I help you?" The coach calls to us as he finally approaches.

"Coach, did you happen to hear what your side of the crowd was chanting at my son?" I ask, that hot flush of heat burning more than ever as the coach looks back at me in silence.

"They were making monkey sounds," my husband adds.

"Are you really going to let that behavior go on in this program?" I ask, thinking of my boys and the countless conversations we have had about respect. What was the point if the world wasn't prepared to show them the same?

Eventually, the coach relented and apologized to Eric and us while issuing a stern reprimand to those who started the offensive chants. In the end, justice was served, but part of me can't help but wonder how much justice would have been served if I had not been there that day. Would there really have been a resolution if I had decided to remain in my chair, or if my husband had not ultimately decided to back me up?

I pray that you develop enough courage to stand up for yourself and those you love. I pray God gives you strength and love to penetrate the walls of hatred that may come up against you and your family. — Sonya' W.

Chapter 5
Picking up the Ball
Stand up When Your People Need You

"It's about leaving something better for our kids. That's how we've always moved this country forward, by all of us coming together on behalf of our children, folks who volunteer to coach that team, to teach that Sunday school class, because they know it takes a village."
--Michelle Obama, as part of her Democratic Convention speech in 2016

It's the end of the season and time to turn in our baseball equipment. Coaches are huddled in the clubhouse with disappointment and confusion etched on their faces. As we prepare to leave, I ask one of the board members what's going on, and he begins to explain that the football president decided not to return, and it was time for the season to start. How horrible of him to quit at the beginning of the season. Who was going to step up?

Unfortunately, all of the board members were baseball people and really didn't have kids playing football, except us. Back at home, my husband and I worriedly talk about the football program's woes, and I ask him if he plans on doing anything about it. "We can't let the kids down," I insist. "Someone has to stand up."

"You should do it," he finally says, and I look at him like he's absolutely crazy. I laugh and walk off. I don't even like football; I don't understand it; how could I ever lead the football organization?

That night, I toss and turn. I can't stop thinking about how we let all of those kids who look like me down, but I don't know a thing about football. The following Monday, the only topic at our bi-weekly board meeting was 'What about football?' When the president asked if anyone wanted to lead the program, no one stepped up, but everyone sure had a lot to say. "Those parents are rude, ghetto," someone said.

"They're horrible and will curse you out," someone else added. I didn't think they could be all that different from the high-strung t-ball parents all over the field trying to take pictures of their kids during the game. More to silence the finance chatter than anything, I finally decide to speak up. "I'll do it," I proclaim. My husband looks at me like he is in shock. "Yea, I'll do it." I had no idea what I was getting myself into.

It was amazing. Once I had agreed to take the lead, every board member in the room offered to join me to help save the program. It wasn't easy. We were at the field every night trying to understand the state of the program.

Where's our equipment?

Why is it so old and raggedy?

Everything was dirty and stinky. Every other light was out on the field, and the grass was so tall it was coming through the bleachers and growing through the fence. The field backed up to a creek, but the kids couldn't use that side of the field because it had become a dump filled with bricks, old fence parts, weeds, and God knows what else. I finally begin to ask why everything is such a mess. That's when everyone starts telling me why the previous president left. He had stolen all of the money, didn't buy equipment for the kids, never invested in refurbishing anything at the park or for the kids. I felt sickened. Despite their amazing talent and undefeated record, our kids were the stepchildren of the league. I remember seeing one of the kids using duct tape to hold his pants up because his parents couldn't afford his football belt, and my heart broke. It broke a little more each and every day. I learned more and more about the disparity in our inner-city organization. We were an Optimist Club. How could we allow this to happen?

Every Monday, we said the pledge and recited the creed "I Promise Myself…." Yet we were only caring for half of the program, baseball, and completely disregarding football. At that moment, I was more determined than ever to turn things around.

It's time for the first football president's board meeting. My vice-president offers to attend with me to help me understand everything that was going on. We arrive, and I'm a little nervous, but I have my clipboard, pen, and paper, and I'm ready-- so I thought. We walk into the room, and it is split like the red sea. The white presidents and VPs are on one side of the room, the black presidents and VPs on the other.

The chair was the head of The North Association and was a pretty nice guy. Right off the bat, he shares how excited he is to see me and begins raking the previous president over the coals, sharing how cheap and mismatched our kids' uniforms always looked. This leads to lots of questions. Because of my membership on our league's board, I knew we had money, but I had no idea where it was all going.

Also, on today's docket is talk of who will be hosting games. This was a great way to raise funds since you could charge two dollars per person. After consulting with my VP, I offer to host two regular season games along with playoffs. Everyone looks shocked, and the hiss of whispers rises up throughout the room, steadily growing into an all-out murmur. I ask the football chair what all the chatter is about. "Well, no one really likes to come to your field because the fields are unkempt, there are no concessions, and the parents are always so rowdy."

"That was the previous president," I declare, looking and feeling a bit insulted. "We'll be ready." All the while, I'm thinking, 'I have no clue how I can pull this all together.'

The very next Optimist board meeting, I make sure I'm on the agenda. I tell them I need money and manpower. We're hosting four games. I'm met with blank stares. I know I'm poised for an uphill battle.

Finally, one football parent who was also a board member interjects. "What do you need us to do?" He asks. "We do everything for baseball. Why we can't do the same for football?"

"But who's going to run concession," the concession boss quickly asks.

"Well, we can get two parents for each home game," I begin, but she squashes the idea before it's fully formed.

"You need to have a board member in there, and I ain't doing it.

It was clear that many of the board members wanted nothing to do with the predominantly black football organization. My next move was to recruit more football parents to become board members. After a month, I had a team of new board members, football parents, and cheerleader parents all behind me, believing in my dream to turn our program around.

I was in the third month, and it was almost time for the season. I was exhausted, sitting in the board room sifting and sorting jerseys. I ordered the best of the best for our kids. I was determined there would be no shame amongst our kids this year. Raising money was indeed a challenge. It was clear that the registration, if paid at all, never made its way to the league's bank account. I took a new approach similar to the school fees. I sent half page letters home, information letters, fees due, and consequence letters. "Your child will not play if you don't either come to apply for a scholarship or pay your fees."

Now, I had to prepare for the influx of parents once word got out that we had scholarships. We would offer half off fees in exchange for concession duty at two home games. I had to leverage every asset I could to put our program together with limited help.

While locking up one night, one of the coaches pulls me to the side, and he begins to tell me how grateful he is for all the work I was doing. The fields look great, he loves the uniforms, and we're actually playing games at home. He asked if the board members and I would be attending games.

"Of course," I reply. "Why would you ask that?"

"Well, in the past, we never had any representation," he says. "So, when something goes wrong, we just roll with it."

I pause and look him in the eyes. "Those days are gone," I say firmly. "We will be there. And not only that, there will be a board member at every game, home and away."

Later, I couldn't help feeling like my stomach was a little queasy. 'Probably skipped dinner one too many nights.' I think to myself. On the drive home, I feel the hot water in my mouth start to overwhelm the rest of my senses, and I know we have to pull over. Suddenly I'm puking on the 2-mile ride home. We pull up in the driveway, leaning over in the car with my head resting on the window, and my husband says, "I think you're pregnant."

"What?" I'm shocked. "With everything going on? No way. I don't have time for that. There is so much to be done. So much work."

I go into the house to lie down. My husband doesn't say a word but pulls out of the driveway and returns fifteen minutes later with a pregnancy kit, and drops it on the bed.

"Here," he says.

Six months later, Alec was born.

But the journey must go on. My work is not finished. My passion is to demonstrate the love and value for all of the children in our inner-city park, creating a safe, loving place for them to escape from their broken homes, fatherless families, so many children who just needed someone to believe in them. This is where the boys were sharing us with 300 other kids and families, standing up for what was right, giving back to the community, passing out hugs, kisses, and cheers for others.

Sometimes, we are the light in the darkness, not so we can see, but so that those around us can. May the Lord grant you the strength to shine brightly enough to give those around you perfect sight.

--Sonya' W.

Chapter 6
Why Are They Over There?
Fight for Your Community

"I am not a perfect servant. I am a public servant doing my best against the odds. As I develop and serve, be patient. God is not finished with me yet."

--Jesse Jackson, in his 1984 speech at the democratic National convention

Like most Saturdays as a board member, my time and attention are constantly needed at our ball park. We're hosting games, running concession, and making sure everything is in order from sun up to sun down. It's fall ball season, and there are games on every field, with over two hundred people in the park. I'm all over the park making sure our umpire crew has baseballs, Concessions has hot dogs, the fields are unlocked, the lights are on by dusk, and the restrooms have toilet paper. Thank goodness for all of the board members on hand helping everywhere.

Looking at my ringing phone, I see four missed calls from the same number. A sinking feeling fills my chest as I answer to hear Coach Jones, head coach of our junior division Mustang football team. Tonight, they are guests at our enemy field in Round Rock. Let's just say the demographic make-up of the teams in this league was the polar opposite of our own, but we have been playing them for years. I'm sure it's one of the common coach complaints -- the officials are cheating us'. Nothing could be further from the truth.

"We need you now," Coach Jones yells furiously. "We need you."

"Wait," I yell back. "Where are you? What is going on?"

He starts to explain, and my mouth drops open in disbelief. Soon I'm gathering the other football board members together, and we're headed for Round Rock.

I can't drive fast enough. My children, my coaches, my parents are all I can think about. Normally, we have board members at every game, but Coach Jones has such a cool head and never has any issues. I knew, though, that if Coach Jones calls, then we load up no questions asked.

So, there we are, on the way to Round Rock, prepared for the worst. Tonight's crew of board members consists of myself (black), Jim (Hispanic), Eric (white), and Tony (Hispanic).

Upon our arrival at the football field in Round Rock, the score is 40-6. We all see what Coach Jones had explained over the phone, and our mouths drop open in disgust. On one side of the field, there are lights, bleachers, restrooms, concessions, and easy access to the field. But across the field, there are no lights, no seats, and a dip in the grass that would be difficult for any of the expecting moms or grandparents to cross. Why? How? I couldn't believe our parents and fans had been summoned to sit across the field in the dark. What in the hell is going on?

Twenty minutes later, the board members and I are fully dressed to make it clear we mean business. We announce that we represent Delwood and need to speak to someone in charge.

"What in the hell is going on?"

"Where are all of their essentials? The ballpark amenities?"

We let the outrage flow from us like a well.

"Where is Mike, your president?" I ask angrily. "I need to speak with him. And I need my parents treated just like everyone else here, or this is over."

Mike arrives a few minutes later, looking bewildered, but I do not intend on showing Mike mercy tonight.

"Mike, I know you know the Delwood parents are sitting across the field in the dark, and I need to understand what is going on."

"Well, your team is cheating," Mike replies. "The game is basically over, and our players don't even want to play anymore."

"What does that have to do with the segregation?" I fire back, and that word strikes Mike.

"Sonya', you know me, it's not like that," he starts to stammer.

"Well, what is it like, Mike?"

By this time, the parents on Mike's side join the conversation and start to express how our players are too big, cheating, and using player tape to choke their players. These crazy comments, of course, insight a reaction from our coaches. Before long, tempers are at an all-time high. Our board members are trying to calm our coaches. Mike is trying to calm his parents. I'm thinking, 'this cannot, I mean cannot turn into a little league football parent brawl.'

Just when it seems things can't get any worse, cool-headed Coach Jones steps in.

"You want to quit?" Coach Jones asks Mike, letting every inch of his six-foot-three frame tower over Mike.

"We'll take our team and go home."

"Are you sure?" I ask, looking up into his face for reassurance.

"Yes," he responds confidently.

We march across the field, get our parents and kids and head back to our home field. I am furious and can't wait for the next Football Presidents meeting on Monday. Prior to the meeting, I spoke with Coach Jones and requested his presence at the board meeting. I want to leave no chance for a misinterpretation of what happened.

Monday

Word has gotten around the league, and every football president and board member is aware of what transpired in Round Rock. The room is filled with everyone talking about what happened, and the meeting hasn't even started. Black presidents and board members are ready to speak their peace, and white presidents sit together discussing and planning. As soon as the meeting begins, the first order of business is the Delwood/Round Rock football fiasco. The president of Round Rock immediately raises his hand and requests to speak. He begins to explain that they have decided their organization cannot compete in our league and would be pulling out. During Round Rock's time with the league, they have yet to win a championship, and the same organizations always seem to win. He never mentions the events from over the weekend.

I'm floored. 'You just gone' sit here and act like we not gone' talk about my parents sitting in the dark across the field?' I think to myself.

Just as I go to speak, good ole faithful, Kris, jumps in.

"So, to simplify what you're saying, is you don't want little Jimmy and Bobby playing with Kareem, Mike, and Kevin?"

Mike turns red, and the conversation quickly escalates into a shouting match. The Round Rock representatives departed the meeting early, and that was the last time we ever dealt with them.

Sometimes for some, it is easier to go on exhibiting racist behavior. There was no justifiable reason for the Round Rock team's actions other than they didn't want the black parents sitting with the white parents, and I knew it. Moments like these are chilling to the very bone as I look at my white husband for clarity.

"Some mother fuckers are just stupid," he says. "Fuck'em". Our kids are the real deal, and they are whooping their ass. But that was some bullshit they pulled."

I'm glad I could count on him as a gauge for whether or not I'm overreacting here.

The meeting begins again, and League President, James, jokes that we need to make some scheduling changes since Delwood can't play nice. We always find a way to laugh, be resilient and make it back about the kids.

"To have long term success as a coach or in any position of leadership, you have to be obsessed in some way."

--Pat Riley

Chapter 7
That's My Husband
When Labels Start Flying, Duck

I'll never forget the summer day our team, Delwood, was scheduled to play an away game at Dove Springs on the other side of town. Things start normally enough. We meet at the usual baseball field to set up carpools and offer rides to kids whose parents wouldn't be able to make the game at all. So, we had about five or six car loads of players (no more than nine or ten years old), coaches, and parents, all in game mode. Before I go on with this story, let me just tell you about Mr. Worden's coaching style. Our team, the Delwood Yankees, was so good people would literally ask, "Are they little robots? They're so focused. So, into the game, and they know exactly what to do." The team won championship after championship with my husband as their coach. Coming in first place for the season was always expected and happened each year without fail.

Fast forward to game day at Dove Springs. We arrive at Dove Springs, and the players hit the field, lay out their equipment, and start drilling like a team of minor leaguers on the cusp of getting called up to the majors. There's no horseplay. They arrive and get right to business. The few of us who traveled are in the stands chatting and awaiting the start of play.

Once the game started, we all knew we had one solitary job to do, and that was to cheer our kids to victory. We aren't interested in coaching from the sidelines. I thought I'd leave that to my husband. Everything started normally enough, except we noticed the umpire appeared to be wearing shorts with leg gear, usually a sign that he was uncertified and likely unfamiliar with the rules of the Pony Baseball League. Now, you would think that would not be a problem, but every league usually has some sort of specific rule adjustment, deviation, or addition to the MLB rule book, which is the foundation of American baseball.

To the surprise of no one, tensions start growing from the third inning on, as Coach Worden notices some frankly bad officiating from our uncertified umpire. Umpire calls are, of course, a matter of judgement, but there are some pretty solid rules regarding tagging up, running through first, remaining in the batter's box, and so on.

It was at the bottom of the third inning that fireworks started to fly. We have a lightning quick runner up to bat in Devin 'Tea Spoon' Collins, the count is 0-2, and the opposing team's fans are having a cheer battle with us as they hope for the out. We know our job, which is to cheer non-stop, win, lose, safe, or out. And believe me, I'm not one to take my job lightly.

I'm on my feet, little Alec in tow, rattling bottles and making as much noise as I possibly can.

The pitch comes, Devin swings, but the catcher drops the ball. Coach yells run, and Devin bolts down the first baseline. Devin is probably one of the shortest kids on the team but has lightning speed, which is very handy on the field. The next batter comes up, and before the pitcher can even get in position, Tea Spoon flies to second. The umpire calls time, the fans are yelling, and we are confused because it was a fair play. The umpire motions Tea Spoon back to first and claims that he hadn't said play ball, so the ball was dead. This did not set too well with Coach Worden, who marched right down the 3rd baseline and gave that umpire a piece of his mind.

After a few minutes delay, the game resumes, and as soon as the pitcher begins his motion to pitch, Tea Spoon, who was already off the first base bag, takes off like lightning. Coach D. on first had given him the green light to get to third and to not stop. It was a sight to see. By the time the ball reached the plate, Tea Spoon was rounding second, and by gosh, by the time the catcher gathered himself to throw to second, Tea Spoon was on third high fiving Coach Worden. The stands go crazy. Our side yells louder than ever, drowning out the moans and groans of the opposite team's fans. Who could have possibly guessed that the very next play would end the game?

Now, with a player on second and third base and with us in the lead, Coach Worden gives the sign for a suicide squeeze.

Now, before you judge, let me just tell you about the regiment of daily team practices, drills, and discipline these boys were put through before getting to this point. You may think, well, they're too young for signs. This was one of the few teams at that age level capable of using signs, and the boys executed on them without fail. The sign to the batter for a suicide squeeze tells the batter, 'No matter what, do not swing the bat'. Basically, you are a statue in that batter's box, and don't you move because the player on third is coming home. At this point, the other team is rattled. What was a strike three ball, has led to a player in scoring position. In the stands, we have no clue what's about to happen, but the coaches and players are so in sync. As soon as the pitcher leans back to pitch, Tea Spoon, already four feet off the bag, jets down the baseline and slides into home, the catcher fumbling with the ball all the while. It was textbook. The kids in the dugout are screaming and cheering, Tea Spoon is glowing, our Coaches are giving each other the look of satisfaction, and parents are jumping up and down, screaming and yelling at the top of their lungs.

And then…the umpire yells for time, points at Tea Spoon, and ejects him from the game. Coach Worden turns five shades of red, with the meanest grimace on his face you ever want to see, points at that umpire and tells him he's a piece of shit who doesn't know the game and should be ashamed to be out here cheating the kids. This time, their argument continues. In frustration, Coach Worden announces that he has had it with the bushwhack team, and we're leaving. Our parents completely agree. We had had enough. We gather our cups, chairs, pom poms, shakers, and snacks. We stand outside the dugout and wait for the players to come out. All of a sudden, the Dove Springs fans decide to come over to our parents and tell us what they think of our Head Coach. One parent in particular really let it rip. "He has anger management problems. He's abusive. I can't believe you let him coach your kids. He should not be around kids." She goes on and on, but we all ignore her. It's not uncommon for this kind of reaction from upset parents in the throes of defeat, after all. Besides, as the coach's wife, it's my duty to be the role model, stay cool, and help the other parents stay cool. But chatty Kathy from the Dove Springs side can't seem to leave well enough alone. She continues with, "y'all shouldn't have to cheat to win. That was a dirty play, and he's racist and shouldn't be around kids."

WAIT!!!!

It was like the world had suddenly gone slow motion as the words R-A-C-I-S-T roll off her tongue. And at that moment, I begin to look around. By this time, the players had started emerging from the dugout, and all I can remember is seeing the glassy look in my son's eyes and saying to myself, 'this B-I-T-C-H done gone too far'. Before I knew it, with Baby Alec still on my hip, I reached over a parent to grab the Dove Springs loudmouth by the head to rip out her tongue.

"My son is on that team, and that's my husband," I yell. "You don't know what the f**k you're talking about. He's not a racist!" That filthy mouth heifer had crossed the line.

"Sonya', nooooo!" Yelled one of the moms from our team. But there's just something about when you reach your saturation point, and someone has inflicted pain on your undeserving children. I had had it with her unfounded insults and accusations. And just like that, something was triggered inside of me. I was done staying cool.

Fortunately for Loudmouth, one of our parents grabbed me and took Baby Alec and me safely to the car while the other team's parents grabbed that heifer. After loading up all the kids, we returned safely to our ball field.

Normally we would wait for all the kids to get picked up and go our separate ways, but this time after getting back to Delwood, we all got out of the car and gathered at the BBQ pit hut. Still in disbelief of what just happened, we begin discussing the horrible calls, the disgusting parent who crossed the line, and the wasted trip. Perhaps since my husband was the only Caucasian on the field, and our team was all children of color, Loudmouth had just assumed that he was Keanu Reeves from "Hardball," giving back to the inner city. Or maybe she thought because he was the only Caucasian on the field that she needed to warn us. Whatever it was, it was the wrong day, wrong team, and wrong family. Now, I know I didn't quite handle that teachable moment the right way, but I got better with time.

This incident would prove to only be the beginning of baseball and racism.

48

May God grant you strength, empathy, and the knowledge to know when to use them.

--Sonya' W.

Chapter 8
The Baseball Card Police
When You Don't Feel Welcome

The weak can never forgive. Forgiveness is the attribute of the strong.
-Mahatma Gandhi

Unless we were playing in the inner-city, I was usually the only African-American mom in the stands for our team, traveling out of town for 3-4 day tournaments. No one even so much as attempted small talk with me until Eric started to thrive as a youth sports pitcher. Suddenly, people who had previously passed over me now would approach and ask if I was Eric's mom and what a great pitcher he was.

I openly shared these observations with my boys on a number of occasions at home and in the car on the way to games. It was important to me that they understood why I always sat alone and did not mingle or make small talk. On occasion, I would overhear parents make comments about minority inner-city teams because they didn't know I was actually part of the team.

Five or six baseball teams later, my son, Eric, is now 17 and excited about making the latest team. He giddily hops on my bed and says, "Mom, our team is having a get to know each other pool party this weekend. Can we go?"

Immediately, I'm sure that I will be the only African-American at the party. Based on the ethnic make-up of many baseball teams before, I don't want to spend my Saturday being the 'only'. So, I decide to say to him, "Oh, you and your dad can go. I'll pass on the baseball parent togetherness, but I'll definitely be there to cheer for you and your teammates."

Eric and I arrive at the field for the first game of the season. We're an hour early, so Eric runs in and joins the team while I sit in the car until its closer to game time. As game time approaches, I stroll through the gate and find the field our team is playing on. I notice an empty area in the bleachers at the top in the corner. It's breezy up there, and I can pop open my umbrella since I'm not trying to get a suntan, unlike everyone else. Other parents are spread throughout the stands. Ten minutes or so before the game is scheduled to get started, the coach comes to the fence and calls a parent over. He hands her baseball cards with our team's roster on them so we can support all of the children. The parent starts passing the cards out to the parents sitting near her. Of course, I don't get a card, but I've never met them, so no problem, I think. I'll just lean down and ask for one.

"Excuse me, can I have 2 of the baseball cards?" I ask.

"Oh, these are for our team," the woman replies.

"Yes, I know," I retort. "My son is on this team."

"Your son is on this team?" She responds, indignation in her voice now. "Our team is on the field right now. What's his name?" She asked this last question pointing at the field as if it was my job to pick my kid out of a lineup.

"I know my son is on this team and on the field right now," I reply, my blood pressure definitely on the rise. "His name is Eric Worden, #12, and he's right there."

Thankfully at this point, my antagonist's husband snatches the cards from his wife and hands a few over to me. "I don't know why my wife is trying to be the baseball card police," he says apologetically.

Some say innocent, some say a mistake, I say who decided that it was your job judgement or assumption that I was not a mom on this team? For all she knew, I could've adopted one of those children.)

That game became the longest seven innings of baseball I have ever watched. I felt angry and wanted to curse that lady out, but I would not dare give her the satisfaction of watching me get kicked out of the complex for being disruptive. So, I sat alone and cheered for my son. Sat in anger as I heard them cheering for my son as well. Finally, the last out, it's time for our routine after every game. I wait for Eric to come out of the dugout, and he greets me by hugging me and kissing me on the forehead before we walk together to the car. Today especially, I could not wait for this moment as it was the only time that I felt like I was supposed to be there.

Dear Lord, we ask for your strength to forgive those who trespass against us.   Free us dear Lord from the hurt and pain that weighs on our heart. In Jesus Name, Amen. – Sonya W.

Chapter 9
Social Media
Make Sure the Kids Get the Message

The truth is, unless you let go, unless you forgive yourself, unless you forgive the situation, unless you realize that the situation is over, you cannot move forward. - Steve Maraboli

I pull out of the office parking lot in a hurry, hoping I'm not late to pick Eric up from practice. My doting pays off as I arrive just in time to scoop him up, his Gatorade and snack in tow.

The ride home is about 20 minutes, and Eric spends it scanning his phone as usual while I fight the evening traffic. I glance over at his phone and notice what appears to be a video playing of a black man being pulled over by a white cop. Normally this probably would not have caught my attention, but this was on the heels of a string of police officers accosting and shooting black men during what initially appeared to be routine traffic stops.

"What's that you're looking at?" I ask him.

"Oh, nothing, mom," he replies in that typical way teens do when they don't want parents prying.

"Let me see," I say firmly before he hands the phone over to me.

"Mom, don't get mad," Eric says, "The video shows a special needs police officer stopping a black driver. The driver asks, 'why did you pull me over?' and the officer says, 'driving while black'.

Immediately, I feel a geyser of anger bubbling up inside of me. "Who sent this to you?" I ask sharply. "This isn't funny. Don't they know that you are biracial and I am black?"

Eric quickly explains that no one had sent the video to him directly, but it had been circulating in the baseball team's group chat. I'm furious and can hardly drive to pick up his brother. As we make our way home, Alec, Eric, and I have a family conversation about the video and how serious this is. Unarmed innocent black men and women are being killed while much of society chooses to look away or even laugh. I share my concern that the next black person who gets shot down could be one of them or one of our relatives. I try to relay the importance of standing up and confronting these situations regardless of Eric's friends' intentions. These situations are wrong and hurtful. And to Eric's credit, he quickly understood.

Later, I sent an email to Eric's coach, who took immediate action by calling a team meeting and speaking privately with the player who sent the video. The next day when I arrived to pick up Eric, he ran to the car and said the player who sent the video wanted to talk to me. My heart is racing. I don't talk to kids. I talk to parents. But maybe I should hear what he has to say. Eyes full of tears, he comes over and apologizes and admits what a mistake he made. He promised he was not racist and would never intentionally do anything to hurt Eric or anyone like that again. He was so remorseful that I got out of the car, and we embraced. For the rest of the year, he couldn't see me without giving me a hug or a big wave and smile. Education and forgiveness are the sweetest mixtures.

God, we ask that your light and love saturate our hearts as we forgive those who persecute us. Although uncomfortable we pray for your discernment and guidance in each and every situation. Amen
— Sonya W.

Chapter 10
Brothers Break Apart
Baseball Betrayal

True forgiveness is when you can say, "Thank you for the experience."
- Oprah Winfrey

They did it!!! They did it!!! I can't believe they did it!!! Everyone is screaming at the top of their lungs. My aunts, uncles, cousins, and scores of friends are here for Alec's final high school game. What an amazing game he had. From a hit up the middle to a defensive marvel in a diving catch to multiple stolen bases, it was Alec's night through and through.

That night, the game starts with a special on-field ceremony. Parents line up on the first base line, and each player is called and brings his mom flowers and thanks her for all the years of support. I can't help the tears streaming down my face as Alec approaches. He's so happy. He's a senior. He's a starting varsity player. What a year he has had.

I turn to all of the family and motion to the field. We get to go on the field and take amazing pictures of the team receiving their district championship trophy.

Tonight's victory clinches the playoff bid and allows Liberty High School's longstanding tradition of playoff competition to continue. This year had been different from years past. Two of the other team moms and I had actually bonded over similarities and concerns earlier in the season. We gossiped, cheered, and even took a picture to remember our time together. We were all so happy that it was over. Friday night lights, so we thought.

I did my best to soak in the adulation that night. All three of my sons had traveled the same baseball path as Liberty High School Knights. Finally, the baby of the family had completed his journey. I could not have been prouder. After everyone had said their goodbyes and gotten their fill of hugs, the boys all decided to ride the school bus back to the school one last time.

And that's when screenshots of a social media post begin to circulate amongst the team. In the screenshot, our starting catcher, Allen, is bragging about his grandfather owning slaves and using the n-word left and right. Everyone had seen the post, and Alec was the last to be shown the screenshot. His heart immediately sank with betrayal as he saw whose social media it was.

Allen was one of Alec's closest friends. In fact, Alec sometimes felt like Allen was his brother inside baseball. So, when Alec saw the social media post in question had come from Allen, it was natural that he would feel hurt beyond belief.

Allen was enraged because a black football player had taken his girlfriend. Take that hurt and add a heavy dose of rousing from the other guys, and you have a very combustible situation. Of course, Allen was going to lash out, and he chose social media as his preferred venue. He never meant for it to be seen, but someone had betrayed his confidence and took a screenshot from the chat group he was in and sent it to the baseball team.

Unaware of all of this, the rest of the parents and I pull up at the school, waiting for the bus to arrive as usual. The kids unload and head to the batting cage for their end of the night huddle with coach. Alec totes his equipment and comes to the car as usual. I probably take more celebratory selfies, and he obliges, not saying a word the entire ride back. I still don't know at the time, but the hurt is literally making him nauseous. After sleeping on it, Alec decides he is going to send the coach a text message with a screenshot of the group chat and share context of the entire situation.

Still totally unaware of the events from over the weekend, I arrive at Liberty High School the following Monday to pick up Alec, only to find the coach approaching my car with Alec nowhere in sight. Now, that makes me nervous. "What did he do?" I think to myself anxiously. "Where is he?" The coach kneels by my window and carefully walks me through the whole thing. He tells me about receiving Alec's text message, about Allen being suspended from school and kicked off the baseball team, about Alec's bravery in being the only member of the team to come forward about this.

My eyes begin to well with tears, and anger fills my soul. Horrible flashbacks to Eric's senior year creep into my mind. Damn IT, again!!!

Alec comes to the car, and I hug him as tight as I can, again feeling guilt and failure that I didn't somehow protect him from the enormous hurt he must be feeling. After a silent ride home, we start talking more about the incident. He wonders what could have happened. After all, Alec had never had any reason to believe Allen could act like this.

"When people show you who they are, believe them," is all I can say back.

Meanwhile, the team needs to spend the next week focusing on playoffs. It's business as usual with that dark, ominous cloud hanging over the team's head.

I receive a message from Sarah Mills, another player's mom. "Hi Sonya'," the message reads. "I'm so sorry about what happened, that must really be hurtful," was the initial theme of the message, but it quickly reversed course. "Do you know Allen's a really good kid and doesn't deserve such harsh treatment and all he has is baseball? He's just a kid that made a mistake, and if you called the coach and told him you forgive Allen, perhaps he would let him back on the team. You know all kids make mistakes, including your son."

Now, this was getting laughable, but I have enough sense not to get into an argument with this one on social media. Prior to this incident, Sarah and I were what I would consider pretty good friends. She worked at a restaurant that my family loved to frequent, and she would commonly come over and pass out hugs. However, this situation revealed another side of Sarah to me, and I found myself needing to take my own advice: When they show you who they are, believe them.

The next morning, Alec and I decided to make a statement to the world on social media. Alec wore his 'Equality' shirt, and I wore 'My Black Is Beautiful' shirt, captioned by a quote from Dr. King, "We must learn to live together as brothers, or we will perish together as fools." I'd be remiss if I didn't also mention that the post was also my subtle final message to Sarah Mills, who followed me on social media.

The team lost the first-round game of the playoffs, and a majority of the team blamed Alec for snitching on Allen. Unbeknownst to us, Alec met with each of the players with concerns and spoke with them one on one. He told them about the importance of equality and fair treatment for all. He told them that there was no place for racism on the team or in this world. He told them that some things were bigger than a baseball game.

Alec kept the conversations to himself for one year until he and I volunteered to be part of a panel at my job titled "How to Talk to Kids About Racism." At my job, I'm a board member in our employee resource group, created to share and teach about the Black experience and help others understand African-American culture. The boys are fully aware of the work I've done in this realm for the past four years. So, when work asked for panel volunteers, I immediately through our name in the hat. We were asked to discuss and share the talk black families have, particularly with our sons. Alec was asked about how 'the talk' made him feel and to share a time he had a chance to be an ally.

During the dress rehearsal, I was fully prepared for him to share the previous year's events the night Liberty High School had clinched playoffs. He passionately shared what happened step by step as I expected. But then, to my surprise, he began to talk about those one-on-ones with the players. My mouth dropped open as tears rolled down my cheeks in disbelief of his courage and independence to stand his ground. What I didn't know was that many of the white players were angry with Alec because they lost the playoff game and wished he hadn't said anything to the coach.

Others had spoken during the panel's run-through, but Alec was the youngest and one of the most impactful speakers. Just like the rehearsal, the live virtual panel's chat was filled with comments on his courage. Sentiments of tears, disbelief and compliments to Alec echoed through the chat.

"Way to Stand Up!"

"You are so courageous!"

"Super Proud of You, Alec."

Alec beamed as I sat, still disbelieving with tear-filled eyes. Then he reached for the keyboard and typed 'thank you' to my co-workers.

"You helped people today," I told him. "You changed lives. You spoke to two hundred people today and told your story. Someone will stand up because you did. Someone will speak up. That's being a true ally."

Dear God, we surrender our broken hearts to you. God give us the strength and hope that we don't have to heal and know tomorrow is a new day. Amen – Sonya W.

Chapter 11
Education System Failures

Prejudice is a burden that confuses the past, threatens the future and renders the present inaccessible. - Maya Angelou

Son, I'm so sorry I didn't protect you. I'm so sorry I brought you here and did not do my research. I'm so sorry I brought you to a school where there are only 4% minorities. But I promise you; you will never have to come back here again."

Those were the words I said to my son as we sat in the Lee High School Board room with all of those sorry, trifling excuses for Assistant Principal and Principals, security, and whoever else. We had been so excited about our long-awaited move to our new home that we missed the signs. After living with in-laws for three years and saving everything we could, we were finally building our dream home. What an exciting time!!! New home, new furniture, new schools for our little family. We moved the summer before the start of school to make sure Brandon, who would be a freshman this year, could play summer ball and meet new friends. Everything was all set. The school year began, and everything seemed normal; all of the kids were getting acclimated to their new school and making friends. And then the sky crumbled.

My husband walks into the room with that somber look on his face that means it isn't good news. "I have to tell you something," he says.

"What is it?" I ask, thinking it's work-related. He reveals the news is actually about Brandon, and he goes on to share that Brandon has been the victim of racism and bullying at school. My mouth drops open, and all I can get out is the usual string of interrogations when I first hear bad news. "By who? When? Where? What the f**k?"

He begins to explain that it actually started in the summer, and Brandon didn't want to say anything. But there was one particular kid on the baseball team of Cuban descent who constantly had it in for Brandon. Apparently, when the team was preparing for a break after practice, this kid's break cheer was "1-2-3 nigger." As everyone put their hands in, he would yell 'nigger', and the team would yell 'nigger' in kind. That was the beginning of a series of attacks. During weight-lifting class, while Brandon was in the locker room, this same little heathen would point to his boxers and say to Brandon, "you are the monkey on my boxers." The last straw was when he apparently threw a tarp stake and hit Brandon in the back. At this point in the story, I'm absolutely done. I'm boiling so intensely from the rage. I'm surprised my husband didn't observe any steam coming out of my ears. But then I realize that Brandon wasn't quiet because he's an introvert; he's quiet because he's being abused by some little piece of trash. At this point, I'm convinced his parents are trash, the school is trash, and the damn coach is trash too! The next morning, I call in sick to work, and I personally drive Brandon to school. I toss and turn the whole night prior; no alarm clock needed.

"Brandon, let's go, son," I say as he throws on his usual school outfit. "You're not riding the bus today. I'm taking you to school, and I need to talk to your principal."

After we get past all of the red tape to see the principal, they take us to a room with an enormous board table. Pleasantries are exchanged before we can finally get down to business. I begin to recite all of the incidents, and, to my surprise, they are fully aware of what has been going on. Apparently, the assistant principal had encountered an emotionally charged Brandon behind the building because he had just dealt with the bully. And what pearls of wisdom did this educator offer my son in his time of need, you may ask? "Walk away."

"WALK AWAY?" I repeat, incensed, infuriated, and completely betrayed by the educators I was supposed to trust with my children's lives. "So, let me get this straight," I say, trying to catch a calming breath. "You know he's being bullied, and all you can cite to me is your policy about anyone in a fight gets expelled; what the hell happened to self-defense? Can my child not defend himself? Furthermore, where the hell are his parents, and why are you not protecting him?"

"Well," one of the administrators says, a look on his face like he just got a game-changing idea. "The only class they have together is baseball. Maybe we can just take Brandon out of baseball and the problem is solved."
"And why in the hell should my child be penalized while the bully gets to stay on the team?" I rage back. Of course, they could not give me any kind of logical response.

I went on to ask about the bully's parents and if the school had even bothered communicating with them. The administrators assured me they had, but I started to feel like they were just feeding the angry Black woman whatever she wanted to hear.

At this point, I realized just how ignorant these backwaters administrators really were, and I needed to go higher. I turned to the side to face my son, to say, "Son, I'm so sorry I didn't protect you. I'm so sorry I brought you here and did not do my research. I'm so sorry I brought you to a school where there are only 4% minorities. But I promise you; you will never have to come back here again." I instructed him to get his things because we needed to go enroll him in another school. I didn't know where and I didn't know how, but I knew we were getting the hell out of there.

After a few phone calls to family members who were more familiar with how to make that happen, we pulled up at

Liberty High School High School. Liberty High School was what we called a 30 30 30, which meant there was no majority. It was one of the most diverse schools in the district. So, after visiting the AISD enrollment office and signing over parental custody to my uncle, Liberty High School would be Brandon's new home away from home. Sometimes the sacrifice to bring peace to your child has no limits. This particular school was thirty minutes past my job and one hour from our dream home, but driving him to school was my responsibility, and after feeling like I completely failed him at one school, there was no limit to what needed to be done to bring him peace and happiness. I was determined that the bully and the administrators would not win. My son will be happy, play baseball and enjoy his high school days. After finalizing all of our paperwork, we received the green light to report to Liberty High School to enroll. It was like the angels were singing. Unbeknownst to me, Brandon's older cousin, Everett, was a senior and a baseball superstar. This would be perfect. He would become an instant role model and would show Brandon the ropes. It took a couple of weeks, but the joy came back to his eyes, his spirit seemed higher, he had a bounce in his step, and he even began to dress like all the other crazy teenagers. I was loving it.

But you know I wasn't finished. I sent a scathing email to the Superintendent of the H.I.S.D. Consolidated school district. He responded with his sincere apologies and actually asked for the opportunity to make it right and take action. As kind of a gesture as that was, enough is enough, and I was not even going to take that chance. We opted to start our new journey at a new school in a different district. We believed it would be a better situation for our children and in the end that turned out to be a better environment for all three of our sons.

We pray for your grace and mercy as we deal with prejudices of others. Vengeance is yours, please keep us from taking matters into our own hands. Amen – Sonya W.

Chapter 12
When Strangers Have Opinions

'Not everything that is faced can be changed, but nothing can be changed until it is faced.' - James Baldwin

There's only one collegiate team in town, and its Alumni Weekend, so there are lots of festivities all over the campus. I'm overjoyed to get an invitation to the game. We decide to go early and hang out at the African-American Alumni pre-game tailgate. My friend and I walk up to the tailgate, and there's music, food, and people everywhere surrounding the Dr. Martin Luther King, Jr. statue. We walk through the crowd, mingling with friends and meeting new people. As my friend introduced me to an acquaintance who was also from Houston, he shared my ties to the Houston area. The guy I just met asks what brought me to Austin; why would I come to Austin over Houston since there aren't enough Black people in Austin. I tell him I was married, and this was my husband's hometown.

"What's your husband's name?" He asks.

"Eric Worden," I tell him.

"   That sounds like a white guy," he immediately replies, and I nod briskly, hoping the interrogation would stop there.

"Ohhhh," he exclaims. "You married the man, you married masa; I can't believe you betrayed our race by marrying a white man after the way they treated us."

I'm speechless. My heart is pounding inside, and I'm angry. I want to check this dude, but I don't want to make a scene.

My friends and a few of the others standing around find the exchange comical.

"Whatever, he was a good man," I reply lightly.

"Leave her alone," my friend interjects. "They're divorced now."

"Good," the guy replies.

What a rude jerk, I think to myself, ready to move around and away from this guy. And we did, going on with the day's festivities. Still, as short as it may have been, the pain from that exchange would stick with me for years to come.

Dear God, we pray for insight, courage and self-awareness as we continue our journey. We pray for your protection, restoration and transformation of hearts. Amen – Sonya W.

Chapter 13
Being an Ally at Work

"Most people don't want to change. They're comfortable and set in their ways. But in order to change, you have to be able to agitate people at times. And I think that's something that's very necessary for us to improve as a country."

--Colin Kaepernick to USA Today in 2016

We are glued to the TV. My sons and I can't stop watching the officer's knee in his neck as life leaves his body before our very eyes. I can't breathe without thinking about his last breath and his calls for his momma, who was already in heaven. In the living room, my body renders limp as I fall into the chair.

"Why? Why?' is all I could say to my children as tears roll down my cheeks. "Some of them don't care about you, and you must always do whatever they say. Never say a word and ask for a lawyer if taken into custody."

"It doesn't matter what we do. They will hurt you. Please obey all the laws and don't give them a reason."

After watching CNN all night, my prayers were different. They included prayers for every single mom of colored children, male and female. "It doesn't matter anymore. Cover them, Sweet Jesus. Cover them, Sweet Jesus. We can't take it anymore. Oh, My God, please help us. They are killing our children before our very eyes. We are helpless, and we need you, Father."

The next morning comes, and I'm still a little numb, but the office keeps churning regardless of my pain, pain, protest, and unrest. Meetings are on the books, projects are in the hopper, and emails need to be read and sent. It's the 'day after', and I'm trying to keep it together as I look at my schedule for the rest of the week. I stare at my computer without really seeing anything as tears roll down my face. I contemplate taking a vacation to deal with my pain, but is there enough vacation possible to heal from this?

As emails begin to pour in requesting this, that, and the other thing, I'm reminded that I'm the only Black woman on the team and likely the only one moved to tears by the grief from this senseless murder. I press on through the day, being present and actively involved in meetings as if everything is okay. When the day ends, I'm exhausted from burying my feelings and wearing a mask. As soon as my day ends, I'm glued to the news. 'What is happening? Have they arrested the officers? How are the protestors? Will we see real change?'

The pain is too fresh, like an open wound. At night I kiss and hug the boys a little differently and begin my prayers again, praying for relief.

Morning comes, and I just can't do it. I decide to take the day off. I email my manager letting them know I don't feel well.

Two days later, thoughts of one of my sons being the next George Floyd won't escape me and are seeping into everything I do. No one on my team has said a word about the gruesome murder that aired on national television. Nor have they said a thing about the protests that are going on all over the world. Every chance I have before, and after work, I'm watching the news to make sure I don't miss a thing. I guess they don't know the Black community is hurting.

Today is the day. I can't pretend that I'm not broken, in grief, and pain. I have decided to write a letter to my manager.

My heart feels so heavy and filled with hurt in light of the recent egregious acts toward African-Americans. I think the hurt and pain are magnified because media availability literally puts you in the moment. Moments like this often leave me filled with inner doubt and belief if "I Am Making a Difference/Will Things Ever Change"? I look at my sons in fear and pray every day each and every time they walk out the door. Usually, I try to mask my feelings, press on, put it in a box, smile through the pain, and bring 110% until it subsides, but the recent events have left me broken and speechless. I value each of you for your forever support and genuine care for my family and me. I felt you deserved my complete transparency. As a company, we often say, "bring your whole self to work" by sharing this email, today is truly a growth moment for me. This moment of openness and sharing paved the way to what would become a place of newfound understanding between the two of us.

After 10 years of being on this team, the dam broke; I needed to share my pain, my loneliness of being the only as I had dealt with one black person being killed after another…each and every time returning to work and getting in the groove, not missing a beat. This time it was different; exhaustion with the system, law enforcement, those who said nothing, those who disagreed with Black America's frustration.

The following Sunday, it's time to get dressed and visit my place of refuge, my place of peace. It is the only place I can go and feel like people there are concerned with what has happened and what is happening to Black men and women in America. Of course, I'm talking about church!

I fit in here. I am a part of this community, and I belong here. My church family saved me. He saves me and keeps me whole after every broken moment in the world. At an early age, raised in the church, I discovered my faith and love for the body of Christ. Church is the reason I love, I forgive, and I understand my enemies and those that have hurt me in countless ways.

Chapter 14
Addressing the Wrong Thing, the Right Way

"Throughout life people will make you mad, disrespect you and treat you bad. Let God deal with the things they do, cause hate in your heart will consume you too."
—Will Smith

My high energy personality often lands me on event planning committees, where I'm often the de facto face of the people. Once a year at work, a team comes together to host a career fair in the cafeteria. The event consists of a representative from every department sitting at a table for three hours with a tri-fold that described their role while answering aspiring employees' questions. Everything is going off without a hitch, and we're nearing finishing time, so instead of standing and greeting the flow of visitors, many of us are sitting around chatting. It isn't abnormal for me to be the only Black woman amongst a group of leaders.

For some strange reason, today's huddle encircles my table, and we're laughing and having a good time. I can't quite remember what quick and witty thing I said, but as everyone begins to laugh, it happens. I see a hand approach my face, and by the time I glance up, I feel the "tap tap" square on the top of my head.

My face turns dead cold, and my neck cocks to the side. Just then, the 'career Sonya" appears on my shoulder and reminds me that 'this is not how leaders address issues.' But the devil was on my other shoulder saying, 'why didn't he pat anyone else on the head? Why did he only pat the African-American girl on the head? Does he think I'm a peon pet, petting me like a little puppy?'

No matter how hard I tried, I was frozen in place. So, I sat there and pretended I had not just experienced the most humiliating moment in my working life, that my soul hadn't just been crushed, that my humanity had not just been violated. By now, I'm sure you've figured out that it wasn't an African-American that patted me on the head, not that it would have changed my reaction. Honestly, it might have been worse because we know the rules about Black women and their hair. As I take down my career fair setup, I'm literally talking to myself, at a complete loss. This guy that I have worked side by side with for years patted me on the head. 'I let my guard down, and this happens," I mutter to myself. 'Maybe my mom was right all along.'

'Oh, heck no' is all I can think as I finally make it to my desk. Thankfully I bump into my best girl at work, and she knows I'm completely flustered and asks what's wrong. While I clear away the day's mess, I'm taking her through the whole event. Her mouth drops open in disbelief.

"You must talk to him," she urges.

"I'm on my way," I reply. I head to his office, deciding I will not walk around and hold this in as if nothing ever happened.

I give a little knock. "Hey, can I have a word with you for a second?" I ask.

"Sure, come on in, buddy," they say cheerily.

'Maybe not when this is over," I think to myself.

"I really value the working relationship we've developed over the years," I start. "But when you patted me on my head in the cafeteria, that was inappropriate, and as a Black woman, I really didn't appreciate it at all."

At first, he looks baffled and completely confused by what I'm saying. "I did?" He asks.
I proceeded to paint the picture of exactly where we were and what we were doing when he did the deed.

"Ahhh, I did!" He exclaims. "Oh my gosh, I'm so sorry. I didn't mean it in any kind of way, but I understand. I really respect you and value our friendship.

He turns really red, and that's when I know he is genuine in his apology, or he is embarrassed to have this conversation. I go on to share that the moment left me feeling demeaned and belittled, and he continues to apologize over and over. In the end, I'm convinced that it wasn't just a boilerplate

'oh crap' response, but a genuine heart-felt apology. When you
have been through some of my experiences, there was no way I
could let this incident go unaddressed. Having the discussion
was a growth moment raising awareness for both of us.

*Thank you, God, for my growth, self-discipline, and courage to endure
and face my temporary moment of embarrassment. I pray you grant us
all continued strength and growth to act and walk in your light as we
face adverse and undesirable life situations. — Sonya' W.*

Chapter 15
Pushing for New Career Opportunities

"I am thankful for all of those who said NO to me. It's because of them I'm doing it myself."
– *Albert Einstein*

As I sit here and think about my twenty-third work anniversary, twelve years in my most recent role, I know this should feel like the high point of my career. But her words often haunt me. Sometimes it gnaws at my soul, and I don't feel like I belong here. Maybe I don't have the aptitude. Maybe I'm the token.

I have been the only African-American on my team since the group began in 2009. For the first six years, I was the only minority. Some days it feels so heavy and lonely that my eyes well with tears, but then I catch myself before anyone notices. For the past three years, I have given 110% trying to achieve the highest annual rating in our organization, 'Outstanding'. I got it once, but it wasn't even the year I did my absolute best, in my opinion. Still, at that moment, I finally felt seen, valued, appreciated. Finally, it didn't feel like a fluke. Maybe she was wrong.

On the heels of my outstanding rating, I start looking at different internal job openings. After my fourth rejection, I'm sitting at the dinner table reflecting on what I'm missing or what I need to do differently. Is it my natural hair? Is my inner-city accent slipping out (we all knew how to language code-switch in the office)? Maybe it just isn't my time as a Black woman?

I can feel my soul melting on the inside. I believe in my company I said to myself over and over. We are inclusive and believe in the value of everyone's uniqueness. But why do I feel completely broken inside? All I can think about is how I can prove the doubting voice that was on repeat in my head wrong. One year after my last rejection, four job opportunities become available. I apply for all of them at the recommendation of my manager. For one of the jobs, the recruiter advises that there are more competitive candidates before interviewing me. I still interview for the three other positions. Preparing for my interviews brings back late-night reminders of studying for college finals, walking around with all of my examples on half sheets of paper, reading in the morning, after bed, in the car, at the hair salon, anywhere I had a moment. Every day when I wasn't in a meeting, I had Jesse Duplantis and Eric Thomas playing on YouTube. Every free moment of the day, I was preparing to do my absolute best.

Interview day is finally here, and everything is running through my head. What if I failed? What if my interview was horrible? How would I face the other leaders that I work with daily? But one video call to my best girlfriend later, and I'm pumped and ready to go. One hour later, I'm done, and the interview felt great. I felt prepared for everything they threw at me. Now I wait.

One week. Two weeks. Three weeks. And finally, there's an email. The hiring plans have changed, and they need permanent managers instead of temporary managers. We also were not going to have to interview again. This is an amazing opportunity to do what I love so much, and it would mean a promotion for me. Since the divorce, the pressure of being a single mom and ensuring I'm able to provide is always at the forefront of my mind. Routinely, I find myself scared to spend a dollar in case one of the kids needs a new backpack, shoes, jeans, or anything. But maybe it's my time, and my blessing was coming.

Week four. No word yet. I'm not sleeping, and I don't really want to socialize. Paranoid thoughts of not making the cut once again creep into my mind. The phone rings, and it's my good friend asking if I have gotten word yet, and I begin to share how everything was extended, and I'm worried about being turned down, my 5th rejection in two years. I feel like a complete failure. What's wrong with me? What did I need to change? Why wasn't anyone telling me?

That's when my friend gave me the best advice yet which was that I should never say I didn't get it, but that I wasn't chosen. "Didn't get it" implied that I missed it, versus "not being chosen" implied that there was a pool and I wasn't selected. If I wasn't chosen, it was their loss, and I should be on to the next opportunity.

Lo and behold, I find three openings in the Human Resources department soon after. The very next day, I emailed the Human Resources manager and asked if I could meet with her to discuss how transferrable my skills might be for the Human Resources role. She agrees my candidacy is strong, so I apply for the job. I can't give up. The odds are forever against my bi-racial sons, and I must teach them never to give up at all costs. "Believe in yourself and keep trying." That's exactly what I had preached to them for the past fifteen years as they tried out for baseball team after baseball team.

I think back, 2020 has been the longest roller coaster. It actually started great with me loaned out in my dream job, filling in for a manager who was out. But just as that opportunity ended one day, the Covid-19 pandemic began in earnest. Add to that the killing of George Floyd, social unrest, and protests across the nation as country after country shut down, and now, as a result of a reorg at my company, there are manager level and higher jobs all across the company. Due to changes in the hiring process, what would normally take three-to-four weeks will now take five-to-seven weeks.

I'm so mentally tired I decide to take a vacation, thinking this will help me escape sitting on the edge of my seat waiting for the phone to ring. But even after vacation, there was still no decision. By this time, my hope is definitely fading, but I know life has shown me I am all I can depend on, and I can't give up.

The demands of an ongoing project have me pulling some late-night hours. I don't mind working in the evening sometimes. It's when all of the other buzz slows down. Just as I'm getting in my flow, my instant messenger lights up. On the other end is the Colorado Site Leader who I support in my current role, and he wants to know if I have five minutes. "Of course," I reply and proceed to call him. The conversation starts as normal, with him asking about me, so I share what I'm working on regarding the project.

"Well, I may have one more thing for you to work on," he says, a twinkle in his voice. He outlines the hiring process the team had gone through, and after careful consideration, he offers me the position I had been waiting months for. 'STOPPPP!' I think to myself, feeling like I passed out with my eyes open. No way! I'm Black; I'm a woman, it never happens for me; I'm a single mom with 2 kids in college. The door doesn't open.

As I sit in the midst of all of my paperwork and files, tears start to roll down my face. I'm screaming, "No, no, no! Really? Oh my God, it's over. It's over!"

"Yes, it's over," Thomas assures me. He goes on to discuss more details, but I'm so jazzed by this revelation I'm not really hearing what he's saying. I'm having an out of body experience. My mind races back to every rejection, every mentor, all of my preparation, studying, mentor meetings, the eighteen-month leadership development program, the twenty-two-course business curriculum I completed, the sleepless nights, the stress of second-guessing myself, the younger female leaders that I was mentoring. It had all led me here and now. I had achieved.

After our call, the praise dance that had been built up in my soul exploded. I stood up with arms stretched to the heavens screaming, 'Thank you Lord' over and over and over. Then before I know it, my heart is racing, tears are flowing, and I need to jump, run and explode. I go to the living room, where there's plenty of space, turn on my gospel music and get my full praise on. Tears won't stop rolling and flashes of

See, the majority of Black moms are the backbone of the family and will do whatever it takes to care for the family, mentally, physically, and spiritually. This breakthrough this new journey will allow me to be the mom I dreamed I could be to provide opportunities for my 2 college-age sons. I begin to think back to my childhood, watching my father, Rev. Frank C Washington, embrace, love, pray, help, and extend olive branches to all. I recognize the diverse circle of friends my children have cultivated as a small mirror of the past. In this moment I realize they had developed an open, loving heart to all, respectful, hardworking and kind. Well rounded, they possess a first-hand social awareness about the racist plagues of this world that some adults couldn't dream of understanding.

I can recall one conversation so vividly. It was a Sunday morning, and the boys and I were on our way to the early morning service at Greater Mount Zion. I asked the boys if they had noticed how respect often partners with outside appearance. Had they noticed how, as they became young men beginning to wear suits, ties, and dress shoes, the elders, the deacons, and pastors of the church greeted them with a firm handshake? Wasn't it a different reaction from when they were boys in blue jeans and tennis shoes? I reminded them that with respect comes greater expectations. I begin to remind them not to mumble, but Alec catches me before I can finish.

"Mom, we know," he says.

"Know what?" I ask.

"How to shake hands with the men at the church," he continues. Eric then adds, "We know when we're with our cousins we speak by nodding our heads and a 'what's up' and when we're with our baseball friends it's a 'what's up dude'."

This became one of those moments where I could step back as a proud mother, marveling at my boys and how they have become seamless products of two cultures that were often at odds with each other. Yet the boys I see every day are also equipped with a sense of understanding and compassion. These are the boys that fill me with a wave of accomplishment every day. Raising them to be the men they are today, that's my grand slam. And moments like these, I feel like I hit it out of the park.

87

When you believe in yourself, every rejection is a time to learn. May the Lord bless you with the knowledge and power to stand up stronger after you fall.

--Sonya' W.

Chapter 16
Paradigm Change

"Sixty-five years have passed, and I still remember the face of young Emmett Till. ... Despite real progress, I can't help but think of young Emmett today as I watch video after video after video of unarmed Black Americans being killed and falsely accused. My heart breaks for these men and women, their families, and the country that let them down—again. My fellow Americans, this is a special moment in our history. Just as people of all faiths and no faiths, and all backgrounds, creeds, and colors banded together decades ago to fight for equality and justice in a peaceful, orderly, nonviolent fashion, we must do so again.

—John Lewis, U.S. congressman, civil rights icon, 2020

I have been committed to speaking up, educating, and calling out racism for what it is with every encounter. The weeks of pain and anguish that surge through my body with the mention of George Floyd's name will never leave our souls. I realize I might not be here for the upbringing of my great-great-grandchildren, and I pray that my sons continue to pass down the deliberate life lessons that took me so long to learn. Growing up and living with your own provides comfort, but it also lacks a key preparedness for our beautifully diverse world. Most often, people focus on what's different as opposed to fostering a judgment-free, open, and loving mindset for all of humankind.

As a final exercise for my leadership development program at work, I remember preparing to present my business case for increasing diversity in the workplace. This meeting was the grand finale. I would speak to a room full of some of our company's most senior leaders, most of whom did not look like me and were predominantly white males. I knew I needed to create a real connection, and I only had eight pivotal minutes to do it. Eight minutes to communicate the value and urgency for my business case to be implemented.

I dreamed about it for weeks and prayed that God would give me the words and wisdom. In the middle of one of these nights, it hit me. The message that would likely resonate with everyone in the room lay within America's sport. The message was hiding in plain sight, somewhere I'd spent the last two decades of my life living and dying with every at-bat. The message was in baseball.

The presentation day finally arrived, and it is just as I imagined it would be. The stadium seating was filled from top to bottom with senior executives responsible for some of our company's biggest successes. Who knew the thing that I knew best would shape the biggest moment in my career?

Finally, I walk to the stage and take my place. "We're going to talk about baseball." I can feel the heads tilting to the side. I can see puzzled faces.

"I know you're wondering, 'what does baseball have to do with diversity'? But walk with me," I say, my plea punctuated by one of my favorite preacher lines. Then I ask how many of them have taken their kids to play little league baseball, and hands shoot up all over the room. Wonderful, just as I expected.

Then I paint the metaphorical picture. A picture of arduous practices, games, and repetition, all designed to hone a team's skills until they are ready to execute and have a great season. I remind them that coming in first is a great feeling at the end of the season, but the ultimate highlight is the announcement of the all-stars and hearing your name called for the all-star team.

"The feeling of accomplishment," I go on. "Knowing that all my hard work is being recognized and I will represent our entire league at a higher level because I have demonstrated the skills and mastery needed to do the job." The audience is laughing, but I know I have them sucked in.

"That's all we want," I say. "We have worked hard, demonstrated the mastery, possess the skills, and just want an opportunity to make the team."
I click the PowerPoint and bring up my proposal to add diversity to the company's core values.

Despite receiving a thunderous round of applause for my presentation along with my peers for their business case, diversity was not added as a new core value. However, following the events of George Floyd, the company made major changes that made it clear that although very few had made the all-star team, it would change by announcing a 5-year plan to increase minorities at the senior level, adding diversity to every job objective for every employee in the company, making considerable public donations to equal justice organizations and delivering a message of unity and black lives matter.

I don't know if this is where my story ends. I certainly hope not. I have fought at work and at home to educate and advocate. I have never felt like the fight was on my behalf, but on behalf of those unable to fight for themselves or those who need another pair of hands going to bat for them. By taking these stands at work and raising my kids, I can only hope that these lessons touch you somehow, while moving our future generations forward until nobody has to feel like the 'lonely only.'

Lord, please protect those unjustly imprisoned not by bars but by a prejudiced world. Please lead our children away from harm and back home to us.

--Sonya' W.

The Author
Sonya Washington

Sonya Washington, a native Houstonite, is a loving and caring mom of three sons. She has also worked in the insurance industry for over 24 years. Balancing the two, she spent many of her sons' early years as the President and board member of their recreational youth league. And as such, she was able to spread her love to not only her kids, but to many others.

Having never met a stranger, Sonya won't be happy if she's not serving and helping others. Her life motto is ***"to forgive yourself and be the change you want to see."*** And a special tribute to #20Deep.

For fun she enjoys watching baseball, supporting her sons and swing dancing. You can follow her on social media at www.instagram.com/Sonya_renee15 and www.facebook.com/Sonya.washingtonworden

For more on this book and online communities around this top, go to www.thelonelyonly.com